This Notebook
Belongs To:

ERNEST CREATIVE DESIGNS

Date: S   M   T   W   TH   F   S   ___ ___ ___

Activity

What Was The Best Part About Your Day?
Draw or Write About It!

I Feel:

Date: S   M   T   W   TH   F   S   ___ ___ ___

Activity

What Was The Best Part About Your Day?
Draw or Write About It!

I Feel:

Date: S   M   T   W   TH   F   S   ___ ___ ___

Activity

What Was The Best Part About Your Day?
Draw or Write About It!

I Feel:

Date: S   M   T   W   TH   F   S   ___ ___ ___

Activity

What Was The Best Part About Your Day?
Draw or Write About It!

I Feel:

Date: S   M   T   W   TH   F   S   ___ ___ ___

Activity

_____
_____
_____
_____

What Was The Best Part About Your Day?
Draw or Write About It!

I Feel:

Date: S   M   T   W   TH   F   S   ___ ___ ___

Activity

What Was The Best Part About Your Day?
Draw or Write About It!

I Feel:

Date: S   M   T   W   TH   F   S   ___ ___ ___

Activity

_____

_____

_____

_____

What Was The Best Part About Your Day?
Draw or Write About It!

I Feel:

Date: S   M   T   W   TH   F   S   ____ ____ ____

Activity

What Was The Best Part About Your Day?
Draw or Write About It!

I Feel:

Date: S   M   T   W   TH   F   S   ___ ___ ___

Activity

What Was The Best Part About Your Day?
Draw or Write About It!

I Feel:

Date: S   M   T   W   TH   F   S   ___ ___ ___

Activity

_____
_____
_____
_____

What Was The Best Part About Your Day?
Draw or Write About It!

I Feel:

Date: S   M   T   W   TH   F   S   ___ ___ ___

Activity

_____

_____

_____

_____

What Was The Best Part About Your Day?
Draw or Write About It!

I Feel:

Date: S   M   T   W   TH   F   S   ___ ___ ___

Activity

What Was The Best Part About Your Day?
Draw or Write About It!

I Feel:

Date: S   M   T   W   TH   F   S   ___ ___ ___

Activity

What Was The Best Part About Your Day?
Draw or Write About It!

I Feel:

Date: S   M   T   W   TH   F   S   ___ ___ ___

Activity

What Was The Best Part About Your Day?
Draw or Write About It!

I Feel:

Date: S   M   T   W   TH   F   S   ___ ___ ___

Activity

_____
_____
_____
_____

What Was The Best Part About Your Day?
Draw or Write About It!

I Feel:

Date: S   M   T   W   TH   F   S   ___ ___ ___

Activity

What Was The Best Part About Your Day?
Draw or Write About It!

I Feel:

Date: S   M   T   W   TH   F   S   ___ ___ ___

Activity

_____

What Was The Best Part About Your Day?
Draw or Write About It!

I Feel:

Date: S   M   T   W   TH   F   S   ___ ___ ___

Activity

What Was The Best Part About Your Day?
Draw or Write About It!

I Feel:

Date: S   M   T   W   TH   F   S   ___ ___ ___

Activity

_____

_____

_____

_____

What Was The Best Part About Your Day?
Draw or Write About It!

I Feel:

Date: S   M   T   W   TH   F   S   ___ ___ ___

Activity

―――――――――――――――――――――――――――――――

What Was The Best Part About Your Day?
Draw or Write About It!

I Feel:

Date: S   M   T   W   TH   F   S   ___ ___ ___

Activity

_____

_____

_____

_____

What Was The Best Part About Your Day?
Draw or Write About It!

I Feel:

Date: S   M   T   W   TH   F   S   ___ ___ ___

Activity

What Was The Best Part About Your Day?
Draw or Write About It!

I Feel:

Date: S   M   T   W   TH   F   S   ___ ___ ___

Activity

What Was The Best Part About Your Day?
Draw or Write About It!

I Feel:

Date: S   M   T   W   TH   F   S   ___ ___ ___

Activity

_____

_____

_____

_____

What Was The Best Part About Your Day?
Draw or Write About It!

I Feel:

Date: S   M   T   W   TH   F   S   ___ ___ ___

Activity

_____

_____

_____

_____

What Was The Best Part About Your Day?
Draw or Write About It!

I Feel:

Date: S   M   T   W   TH   F   S   ___ ___ ___

Activity

What Was The Best Part About Your Day?
Draw or Write About It!

I Feel:

Date: S   M   T   W   TH   F   S   ___ ___ ___

Activity

_____

_____

_____

_____

What Was The Best Part About Your Day?
Draw or Write About It!

I Feel:

Date: S   M   T   W   TH   F   S   ___ ___ ___

Activity

What Was The Best Part About Your Day?
Draw or Write About It!

I Feel:

Date: S   M   T   W   TH   F   S   ___ ___ ___

Activity

What Was The Best Part About Your Day?
Draw or Write About It!

I Feel:

Date: S   M   T   W   TH   F   S   ___ ___ ___

Activity

_____

_____

_____

_____

_____

What Was The Best Part About Your Day?
Draw or Write About It!

I Feel:

Date: S   M   T   W   TH   F   S   ___ ___ ___

Activity

_____
_____
_____
_____

What Was The Best Part About Your Day?
Draw or Write About It!

I Feel:

Date: S   M   T   W   TH   F   S   ___ ___ ___

Activity

What Was The Best Part About Your Day?
Draw or Write About It!

I Feel:

Date: S   M   T   W   TH   F   S   ___ ___ ___

Activity

_____

_____

_____

_____

What Was The Best Part About Your Day?
Draw or Write About It!

I Feel:

Date: S   M   T   W   TH   F   S   ___ ___ ___

Activity

What Was The Best Part About Your Day?
Draw or Write About It!

I Feel:

Date: S   M   T   W   TH   F   S   ___ ___ ___

Activity

_____
_____
_____
_____

What Was The Best Part About Your Day?
Draw or Write About It!

I Feel:

Date: S   M   T   W   TH   F   S   ___ ___ ___

Activity

_____
_____
_____
_____

What Was The Best Part About Your Day?
Draw or Write About It!

I Feel:

Date: S   M   T   W   TH   F   S   ___ ___ ___

Activity

What Was The Best Part About Your Day?
Draw or Write About It!

I Feel:

Date: S   M   T   W   TH   F   S   ___ ___ ___

Activity

_____

_____

_____

_____

What Was The Best Part About Your Day?
Draw or Write About It!

I Feel:

Date: S   M   T   W   TH   F   S   ____ ____ ____

Activity

_____

_____

_____

_____

What Was The Best Part About Your Day?
Draw or Write About It!

I Feel:

Date: S   M   T   W   TH   F   S   ___ ___ ___

Activity

What Was The Best Part About Your Day?
Draw or Write About It!

I Feel:

Date: S   M   T   W   TH   F   S   ___ ___ ___

Activity

_____

_____

_____

_____

What Was The Best Part About Your Day?
Draw or Write About It!

I Feel:

Date: S   M   T   W   TH   F   S   _____ _____ _____

Activity

_____

_____

_____

_____

What Was The Best Part About Your Day?
Draw or Write About It!

I Feel:

Date: S   M   T   W   TH   F   S   ___ ___ ___

Activity

―――――――――――――――――――――――――――――――――

What Was The Best Part About Your Day? Draw or Write About It!

I Feel:

Date: S   M   T   W   TH   F   S   ___ . ___ ___

Activity

─── **Activity** ───

What Was The Best Part About Your Day?
Draw or Write About It!

I Feel:

Date: S   M   T   W   TH   F   S   ___ ___ ___

Activity

What Was The Best Part About Your Day?
Draw or Write About It!

I Feel:

Date: S   M   T   W   TH   F   S   ___ ___ ___

Activity

What Was The Best Part About Your Day?
Draw or Write About It!

I Feel:

Date: S   M   T   W   TH   F   S   ___ ___ ___

Activity

_____
_____
_____
_____

What Was The Best Part About Your Day?
Draw or Write About It!

I Feel:

Date: S   M   T   W   TH   F   S   ___ ___ ___

Activity

What Was The Best Part About Your Day?
Draw or Write About It!

I Feel:

Date: S   M   T   W   TH   F   S   ___ ___ ___

Activity

What Was The Best Part About Your Day?
Draw or Write About It!

I Feel:

Date: S   M   T   W   TH   F   S   ____ ____ ____

Activity

_____
_____
_____
_____

What Was The Best Part About Your Day?
Draw or Write About It!

I Feel:

Date: S   M   T   W   TH   F   S   ___ ___ ___

Activity

What Was The Best Part About Your Day?
Draw or Write About It!

I Feel:

Date: S   M   T   W   TH   F   S   ___ ___ ___

Activity

What Was The Best Part About Your Day?
Draw or Write About It!

I Feel:

Date: S   M   T   W   TH   F   S   ___ ___ ___

Activity

What Was The Best Part About Your Day?
Draw or Write About It!

I Feel:

Date: S   M   T   W   TH   F   S   _____ _____

Activity

_____

_____

_____

_____

What Was The Best Part About Your Day?
Draw or Write About It!

I Feel:

Date: S   M   T   W   TH   F   S   ___ ___ ___

Activity

What Was The Best Part About Your Day?
Draw or Write About It!

I Feel:

Date: S   M   T   W   TH   F   S   ___ ___ ___

Activity

What Was The Best Part About Your Day?
Draw or Write About It!

I Feel:

Date: S   M   T   W   TH   F   S   ___ ___ ___

Activity

What Was The Best Part About Your Day?
Draw or Write About It!

I Feel:

Date: S   M   T   W   TH   F   S   _____ _____ _____

Activity

What Was The Best Part About Your Day?
Draw or Write About It!

I Feel:

Date: S   M   T   W   TH   F   S   ___ ___ ___

Activity

What Was The Best Part About Your Day?
Draw or Write About It!

I Feel:

Date: S   M   T   W   TH   F   S   ___ ___ ___

Activity

_____
_____
_____
_____

What Was The Best Part About Your Day?
Draw or Write About It!

I Feel:

Date: S   M   T   W   TH   F   S   ___ ___ ___

Activity

_____

_____

_____

_____

What Was The Best Part About Your Day?
Draw or Write About It!

I Feel:

Date: S   M   T   W   TH   F   S   ___ ___ ___

Activity

What Was The Best Part About Your Day?
Draw or Write About It!

I Feel:

Date: S   M   T   W   TH   F   S   ___ ___ ___

Activity

_____
_____
_____
_____
_____

What Was The Best Part About Your Day?
Draw or Write About It!

I Feel:

Date: S   M   T   W   TH   F   S   ___ ___ ___

Activity

What Was The Best Part About Your Day?
Draw or Write About It!

I Feel:

Date: S   M   T   W   TH   F   S   ___ ___ ___

Activity

What Was The Best Part About Your Day?
Draw or Write About It!

I Feel:

Date: S   M   T   W   TH   F   S   _____ _____ _____

Activity

What Was The Best Part About Your Day?
Draw or Write About It!

I Feel:

Date: S   M   T   W   TH   F   S   ___ ___ ___

Activity

What Was The Best Part About Your Day?
Draw or Write About It!

I Feel:

Date: S   M   T   W   TH   F   S   _____ _____

Activity

What Was The Best Part About Your Day?
Draw or Write About It!

I Feel:

Date: S   M   T   W   TH   F   S   ___ ___ ___

Activity

_____

_____

_____

_____

What Was The Best Part About Your Day?
Draw or Write About It!

I Feel:

Date: S   M   T   W   TH   F   S   ___ ___ ___

Activity

What Was The Best Part About Your Day?
Draw or Write About It!

I Feel:

Date: S   M   T   W   TH   F   S   ___ ___ ___

Activity

What Was The Best Part About Your Day?
Draw or Write About It!

I Feel:

Date: S   M   T   W   TH   F   S   ___ ___ ___

Activity

What Was The Best Part About Your Day?
Draw or Write About It!

I Feel:

Date: S   M   T   W   TH   F   S   ___ ___ ___

Activity

_____
_____
_____
_____
_____

What Was The Best Part About Your Day?
Draw or Write About It!

I Feel:

Date: S   M   T   W   TH   F   S   ___ ___ ___

Activity

_____
_____
_____
_____

What Was The Best Part About Your Day?
Draw or Write About It!

I Feel:

Date: S   M   T   W   TH   F   S   ___ ___ ___

Activity

What Was The Best Part About Your Day?
Draw or Write About It!

I Feel:

Date: S M T W TH F S ___ ___ ___

Activity

What Was The Best Part About Your Day?
Draw or Write About It!

I Feel:

Date: S   M   T   W   TH   F   S   ___ ___ ___

Activity

What Was The Best Part About Your Day?
Draw or Write About It!

I Feel:

Date: S   M   T   W   TH   F   S   ___ ___ ___

Activity

What Was The Best Part About Your Day?
Draw or Write About It!

I Feel:

Date: S   M   T   W   TH   F   S   ___ ___ ___

Activity

What Was The Best Part About Your Day?
Draw or Write About It!

I Feel:

Date: S   M   T   W   TH   F   S   ___ ___ ___

Activity

What Was The Best Part About Your Day?
Draw or Write About It!

I Feel:

Date: S M T W TH F S ___ ___ ___

Activity

_____
_____
_____
_____

What Was The Best Part About Your Day?
Draw or Write About It!

I Feel:

Date: S   M   T   W   TH   F   S   ___ ___ ___

Activity

What Was The Best Part About Your Day?
Draw or Write About It!

I Feel:

Date: S   M   T   W   TH   F   S   ___ ___ ___

Activity

What Was The Best Part About Your Day?
Draw or Write About It!

I Feel:

Date: S   M   T   W   TH   F   S   ___   ___   ___

Activity

What Was The Best Part About Your Day?
Draw or Write About It!

I Feel:

Date: S M T W TH F S ___ ___ ___

Activity

What Was The Best Part About Your Day?
Draw or Write About It!

I Feel:

Date: S   M   T   W   TH   F   S   ___ ___ ___

Activity

What Was The Best Part About Your Day?
Draw or Write About It!

I Feel:

Date: S M T W TH F S ___ ___ ___

Activity

What Was The Best Part About Your Day?
Draw or Write About It!

I Feel:

Date: S   M   T   W   TH   F   S   ___ ___ ___

Activity

What Was The Best Part About Your Day?
Draw or Write About It!

I Feel:

Date: S M T W TH F S _____ _____ _____

Activity

_____
_____
_____
_____

What Was The Best Part About Your Day?
Draw or Write About It!

I Feel:

Date: S   M   T   W   TH   F   S   ___ ___ ___

Activity

What Was The Best Part About Your Day?
Draw or Write About It!

I Feel:

Date: S M T W TH F S ___ ___ ___

Activity

What Was The Best Part About Your Day?
Draw or Write About It!

I Feel:

Date: S   M   T   W   TH   F   S   _____ _____ _____

Activity ————

_____
_____
_____
_____

What Was The Best Part About Your Day?
Draw or Write About It!

I Feel:

Date: S   M   T   W   TH   F   S   ___ ___ ___

Activity

What Was The Best Part About Your Day?
Draw or Write About It!

I Feel:

Date: S   M   T   W   TH   F   S   ___ ___ ___

Activity

_____

_____

_____

_____

What Was The Best Part About Your Day?
Draw or Write About It!

I Feel:

Date: S   M   T   W   TH   F   S   ___ ___ ___

Activity

What Was The Best Part About Your Day?
Draw or Write About It!

I Feel:

Date: S   M   T   W   TH   F   S   ___ ___ ___

Activity

_____

_____

_____

_____

What Was The Best Part About Your Day?
Draw or Write About It!

I Feel:

Date: S   M   T   W   TH   F   S   ___ ___ ___

Activity

What Was The Best Part About Your Day?
Draw or Write About It!

I Feel:

Printed in Great Britain
by Amazon